KETTLEBELL TRAINING

Exercises and Training Plans to Sculpt Your Body

(How to Get Stronger, Build Muscle With Exercises)

Allen Mathis

Published by Tomas Edwards

© **Allen Mathis**

All Rights Reserved

Kettlebell Training: Exercises and Training Plans to Sculpt Your Body (How to Get Stronger, Build Muscle With Exercises)

ISBN 978-1-990268-63-2

All rights reserved. No part of this guide may be reproduced in any form without permission in writing from the publisher except in the case of brief quotations embodied in critical articles or reviews.

Legal & Disclaimer

The information contained in this book is not designed to replace or take the place of any form of medicine or professional medical advice. The information in this book has been provided for educational and entertainment purposes only.

The information contained in this book has been compiled from sources deemed reliable, and it is accurate to the best of the Author's knowledge; however, the Author cannot guarantee its accuracy and validity and cannot be held liable for any errors or omissions. Changes are periodically made to this book. You must consult your doctor or get professional medical advice before using any of the suggested remedies, techniques, or information in this book.

Upon using the information contained in this book, you agree to hold harmless the Author from and against any damages, costs, and expenses, including any legal fees potentially resulting from the application of any of the information provided by this guide. This disclaimer applies to any damages or injury caused by the use and application, whether directly or indirectly, of any advice or information presented, whether for breach of contract, tort, negligence, personal injury, criminal intent, or under any other cause of action.

You agree to accept all risks of using the information presented inside this book. You need to consult a professional medical practitioner in order to ensure you are both able and healthy enough to participate in this program.

Table of Contents

INTRODUCTION 1

CHAPTER 1: HOW TO CHOOSE YOUR KETTLEBELLS 4

CHAPTER 2: UPPER BODY KETTLEBELL EXERCISES 7

CHAPTER 3: HOW TO CHOOSE YOUR KETTLEBELLS 11

CHAPTER 4: KETTLEBELLS BEGINNER'S WORKOUT 33

CHAPTER 5: 30 DAY KETTLEBELL WOD EXERCISES 45

CHAPTER 6: DIFFERENT KETTLE BELL EXERCISES 53

CHAPTER 7: EXERCISE TOOLKIT 61

CHAPTER 8: MISTAKES TO AVOID 68

CHAPTER 9: KETTLEBELL SLINGSHOT 73

CHAPTER 10: FOUNDATIONAL MOVEMENT CUES AND TERMS 80

CHAPTER 11: 30 DAYS PROGRAM 85

CHAPTER 12: INTERMEDIATE KETTLEBELL WORKOUTS 99

CONCLUSION 123

Introduction

Kettlebell is one of the exercises that most people regard as cool and interesting. If you have not seen a kettlebell before, you may be curious how it looks like. Well, it's pretty straightforward. It is a black cannonball with a handle that is cast of iron. While there are so many other workout tools that you can employ to achieve your health goals, kettlebell training has many unique health benefits if you choose to incorporate it into your workout routine.

Part of what makes kettlebells exercises mystical lies in its origin. They were popularized in Russia in the 18th century. During this time, the kettlebell was used as counterweights when measuring things like cereals and other dry products.

Soon enough, the farmers started challenging each other to lift the heaviest kettlebells and eventually, they found their way into the hands of strong circus men. After the Second World War, the Soviet Red Army took up the kettlebells in training their soldiers

and later in the 1970s, lifting kettlebells was declared an official sport.

While kettlebells have been around in the US for over a century, they have enjoyed its fair share of resurgence and eventually found their way into the gym and fitness stores. It comprises a bell, a handle, and horns. The bell, in this case, refers to the round cannonball shaped weight, and the handle is what connects the kettlebell by simply sloping downwards on each end, hence referred to as the horns.

It is this design that makes the kettlebell quite a unique tool. You may be thinking "what is the difference between kettlebells and dumbbells?" Well, one thing that you have to take note of is that unlike the dumbbells in which the handle connects two weights that are evenly distributed and lies at the center of them, the kettlebell's center of gravity is usually offset from its handle. This is mainly because it rests several inches away from the center.

It is also important to note that with a kettlebell, it is quite easy to grasp it by the handle, bell end or horns. It is the mainstay to grip the kettlebell by its handle. However, when it comes to certain exercises like squats, it is much easier to grasp them by the horns. To achieve a greater grip on certain poses like rowing, it may be better if you hold the kettlebell by the bell itself. This is

because it will help force the hand to squeeze harder to prevent slipping.

Chapter 1: How To Choose Your Kettlebells

Choosing your kettlebell(s) is really important in order to get the greatest results. If you pick a kettlebell too heavy or too light you will not get that great of a workout that will force you to push yourself. Before I recommend the right kettlebell for you, let me just say that everyone is different, so I can tell you specific the right weight for you, but I can give you a couple of guidelines that will help you make that choice.

Choose At least Two Weights – I recommend you get two different kettlebell weights because you will typically be performing two different kettlebell exercises. Some are going to involve fast explosive movement, where as other will involve slower, more controlled movements. So get one kettlebell weight at least 5 to 10 heavier than the other one. Although this isn't really necessary, it's just a recommendation that I personally use. You can certainly only use one kettlebell at first, whatever you find most fitting for you.

Choosing the right weight – This one is going to be different for everyone, but my recommendation, depending on your fitness ability is going to be a kettlebell weight of 35 pound for men and a 18 pound kettlebell for women. If you are going to buy a second kettlebell then just buy a kettlebell that is 5 to 10 pounds heavier.

But the best way to know the right weight for you is to try out the weight before you buy it. You will generally know if the weight is right for you if you can hold the weight out in front of you for at least a couple of seconds, with your arm out straight. But like I said everyone is different. Get a feel for each kettlebell weight that you can to determine a good for that's right for you.

How To Make Your Own Kettlebell

If you have ever taken a look at the price of kettlebells, you realized that they can get pretty expensive. But you really don't need to buy one, you can easily make your own. There are actually a couple of ways to do this. One way that I found to be the easiest and most cost effective (Found in this Youtube video - https://www.youtube.com/watch?v=Zq9Yxn5a9D8) will cost about $10, considering you already have a few plates laying around. And as you will see in the video you can take it practically anywhere.

Although his necessarily doesn't look exactly like a kettlebell, it will give you the same exalt benefits. In some ways the t bar is actually better than regular kettlebells because of its portability and also your ability to change the weight to your desire.

Here is a more detailed guide to show you how to make it and what to buy at the hardware store - http://www.instructables.com/id/T-Handle-Kettlebell/

Chapter 2: Upper Body Kettlebell Exercises

Jerk Press (Shoulders)

– Start by holding the handle of a kettlebell with one hand. Clean, i.e., lift, the kettlebell by pulling it up to the shoulder of your holding hand while extending through the hips and legs. Be careful to rotate your wrist while you execute this movement, i.e., the palm should eventually face towards ahead of you. This will be your beginning position.

– Keeping your upper body upright, dip your body by bending at your knees.

– Then, quickly change direction by driving your heels through the ground to jump in order to create momentum. While doing so, press the kettlebell above you by extending your arm until lockout. You must use your body's momentum to effectively do this.

– As you go back to the ground, receive the weight back by immediately assuming a squatting position underneath the kettlebell as soon as your feet hit the ground. Landing on your forefoot – or the balls of your feet and not the heel – and immediately letting yourself go to a squatting position will help you minimize foot and knee injuries through optimal shock absorption.

– Go back to a standing position then lower the kettlebell back to your shoulders. This completes one repetition.

– Perform 8 to 10 repetitions per arm/shoulder per set.

Jackknife Pull Over (Abdominals)

– To begin, lie down on your back on the floor. Extend your legs fully with both heels touching each other. Use both hands to hold the larger part of the kettlebell and fully extend your arms all the way to behind the head. You should have formed a straight line with your body by then.

– Begin the movement by "crunching" up, i.e., lifting up one leg and both hands off the floor simultaneously towards each other. The top of the movement should have your shoulder blades off the floor and your hands and knee close to touching each other. As you execute this movement, make sure to exhale.

– Gradually return to the starting position and inhale while doing so.

– Repeat the movement, this time lifting the other leg. That constitutes one repetition. Perform 8 to 10 repetitions per set.

One-Arm Close Chest Press (Chest)

– Lie on your back on the ground, a flat bench, or an exercise mat.

– Hold a kettlebell with one hand and position your hand at the level of your nipple and your arm at a 90-degree bend.

– While keeping your body stable using your free arm and legs, push the kettlebell up until your elbows stop short of locking out.

− Lower the kettlebell to the starting position gradually − that's 1 repetition. Perform 8 to 10 repetitions per arm per set.

Single-Arm Closed Row (Back)

− Position a kettlebell just in front of your feet.

− Slightly bend your knees and extend your butt as far back as you can to bend over and assume the starting position. Keep your lower back straight at all times to minimize risk of injuring it.

− With one hand, hold the kettlebell and pull it all the way up to your tummy and as you do, push your elbow as far back as possible and retract your shoulder blade. Again, always keep your lower back straight.

− Bring the kettlebell down without letting go and repeat. Do 8 to 10 repetitions per arm per set.

Chapter 3: How To Choose Your Kettlebells

Now that we know so much about the kettlebell's past and evolution through time, recognize that if you are getting one, you are now a major part of history. One of the major issues with buying exercise equipment goes back to the one-size-fits-all theory. Many people will just walk down the aisle or showroom of their local sporting goods store and pick out the first piece of equipment that they see. They have done no research on what exercise equipment they will need based on their body types, strengths, limitations, and interests. All of these factors must be considered in order for exercise equipment to be adopted for the long term.

What's even worse, is that people will buy something online, but have no way of testing if it's right for them. When something arrives and not the correct fit, it simply gets discarded. I don't want you to do this with the kettlebell. I want you to take your time, get familiarized, and purchase the one that is best for you. I will not condone impulse buying here. There is a great amount of variety in these pieces of equipment and you will notice this when you try out several different kinds.

Think of it like a bowling ball. When you go bowling, you generally do not pick up a random ball and start hurling it across the lane. If you do, you have probably not been very successful. In order to play well, you need to find the right ball with the correct size holes that your fingers can easily slip in and out of. Plus, you have to find the right weight that feels comfortable for you. For some people, color is also important. How do you know which kettlebell is right for you? Let's find out.

ANATOMY OF A KETTLEBELL

The basic anatomy of a kettlebell is simple. They are cylindrically shaped with an attached handle. Beyond this, the kettlebell differs in the many different shapes and sizes it comes in. The majority of kettlebells are stainless steel or cast-iron as these materials are less likely to wear down. Vinyl-coated kettlebells are also available for those who choose. Some even come with unique designs like those with a gorilla face. Finally, kettlebells with an adjustable handle are an option too.

These details may not seem like a big deal upfront, however, they can make a huge difference when using for various exercises. It is important to feel comfortable with your kettlebell to get maximum results and feel safe. The last thing I want is for you to get one that doesn't feel right and you end up hurting yourself.

There are a few simple exercises that can be performed with any type of kettlebell. These exercises involve very simple movements that require very little interaction with the actual kettlebell. Single-arm deadlifts, single-leg deadlifts, and the slingshot are just a few workouts that can be done, no matter what type of kettlebell you have. If your plan is to stick with these rudimentary exercises, then the decision may not be that important. Beyond this, the choice you make is crucial, especially if you want to do some extreme workouts, which I hope you eventually will. To sum it up, the classic kettlebell looks like a small cannonball with a handle.

THE BEST KETTLEBELL FOR YOU

When choosing a kettlebell, it is important to get one that won't damage your wrists, forearms, elbows, or shoulders. You will be using these body parts throughout almost all exercises so great care must be taken. Also, these weights with the wrong handles can cut up your hands badly. The two best types of kettlebells on the market are the competition kettlebells and the cast-iron kettlebells. Either of these will offer tremendous benefits for you if you are to take your training seriously.

Competition kettlebells have uniform dimensions across all weights. This means that the kettlebell will be the same size at the cylinder and the handle, whether it is 8 kg or 16 kg. In many cases, competition types are separated by colors based on international standards. The particular color of the object will signify the weight. These types of kettlebells last long too due to being made of steel. They are a great option if you plan on taking competition seriously.

The advantage that the competition kettlebell gives you is the consistency between training and competition. While training with a competition kettlebell, you can experience how it feels in your hands and on your wrists. This will be the same feeling you have when using any type of competition kettlebell. Despite what weight the equipment is, it will be easy to get used to because the size will not change. In any type of professional sport, athletes get as acclimated as possible to the environment they will be competing in, plus the equipment they will be using. For example, track runners will try to run the track they will be using in competition as much as possible. This is the same type of advantage you get with competition kettlebells. It is similar to having a home-field advantage.

These types of kettlebells also have small handles with limited space in between. This prevents your hand from sliding side to side, which significantly prevents skin burns and blisters. The disadvantage here is that only one hand will fit on the handle. Unless you are lucky enough to have small hands. I mean very, very small hands. Many important kettlebell exercises require two hands, and with the competition kettlebell, these are not possible. This means your workout routine will be severely limited because of numerous valuable exercises that are out of the question.

It's okay though because you can still get a great workout. However, if you want more variety, we have another great option. Cast iron kettlebells are produced with one solid piece of metal that is uniform throughout. So, the physical size of the kettlebell changes based on weight, unlike the competition kind. This can make it difficult to maintain consistency between training and competition. If your goal is not competition it may not be a big deal to you.

The cast iron kettlebell also offers wider handles which will increase the diversity of the workout routines at your disposal. You will now be able to use two hands, which is especially great when starting out, as many new routines also require both hands to perform. The cast iron kettlebell may be a better option for you if you're a beginner because of the multiplicity in usage it provides. Plus, learning the basics of this piece of the kettlebell, in general, requires two hands, so if you use a competition kettlebell from the start, your foundation will not be solid. This can cause problems for you later on. Not only will you not work out to your full potential, but you will also risk major injury. If you are a newbie, stick with the cast iron for now.

For experienced users, the competition kettlebell is a great option. Make the transition from cast iron to the competition when you feel comfortable and you will be able to incorporate many more exercises. However, when you make the shift, both options can be utilized to get the most diverse workouts in as possible. Overall, when you are ready to take your kettlebell training to the next level, the competition kettlebell is the way to go.

The next major consideration you need to make is the weight of the kettlebell that's right for you. Just like with any other workout, it is important to start off slow and progress as tolerated to prevent unnecessary pain and injuries. The standard weights for kettlebells are 8 kg, 12 kg, 16 kg, 24 kg, and 32 kg. Since the kettlebell has taken off in popularity over the past few years, there are numerous weights in between these numbers that are available too. However, as someone who has used the kettlebell for many years, and teaches classes on a regular basis, I can honestly say that I've rarely used any weights outside of the standard numbers.

There are different weight recommendations between men and women. For this particular book, we will focus on men. In most cases, with weight training, it is better to start off light. With Kettlebells, it is actually better to go with a weight a bit heavier than you think you can handle. This way, you can work on technique and build strength without outgrowing the starting size too quickly. Still, be cautious with the weight and do what you're comfortable with. The last thing I want is for you to get injured because you moved up too fast.

In general, I recommend first-timers to try weights between eight and 16 kilograms. Check these out and see how you feel. If you are experienced with lifting weights and feel like you can handle more, try the 20 or 24-kilogram weights instead. Assess yourself and see how you feel. You know yourself better than anybody. There is no exact science to it. One thing to take into consideration is the units. For those of you not familiar with kilograms, just multiply the number by 2.2 and you will have the weight in pounds. For example, 8 kg x 2.2 is 17.6 pounds already.

Many people will compare kettlebell lifting to dumbbell lifting. Kettlebells are not dumbbells though. While lifting a certain weight may be too much with dumbbell exercises, the kettlebell workouts require a different technique. With dumbbells, you are isolation specific muscles. For example, with curls, you are mainly targeting the biceps and only using this muscle for the most part. This means you can handle less weight. With kettlebell workouts, like swings, snatches, and cleans, you will utilize multiple muscle groups. In this manner, the higher weights are easier to handle because of the greater support. It is analogous to four or five people lifting a couch, versus just one or two. As an example, with the aforementioned exercises, you use your entire upper body, legs for power, and your core to prevent you from getting twisted up.

A major concern that is often overlooked is the handle of the kettlebell. It is an essential part of the tool as that is what you're holding onto the whole time for almost every exercise. Yet, people do not take this area into consideration. The last thing you want is a blistered and bloody hand because of a design flaw. When you do countless repetitions with a poorly designed handle, that is exactly what you will get. With dumbbells, the bar does not move very much, so this is not a major consideration. With the kettlebell, your hands will be moving, sliding back and forth, and side-to-side constantly. If the handles have rough edges, your hands will hate you by the end of the first workout.

Many people will wear gloves for extra protection. This is definitely an option but can interfere with your technique. It is better to just pay extra attention to the handle so you won't have major issues from the beginning. Assess the handle all the way around, including the underside. Make sure it is smooth without any rough edges. The handle may cause some discomfort regardless, but eventually, you will develop some callouses.

The handle should also be the appropriate size and thickness for proper gripping. It should also have adequate space between the handle and the bell. If this space is too small, your knuckles will graze the bell constantly, which will wear down your skin and cause more cuts and blisters. It can also lead to major hand injuries. There is definitely a balance you need to find here. The handle should be sanded down and smooth, but not too smooth; otherwise, you will have a poor grip. This is especially true after several reps, and your hands start getting sweaty. You do not want to let the kettlebell fly out of your hands. Once again, you can use gloves, but it's better to avoid them if you can.

I get that people want to save money. I certainly don't expect you to spend your life's savings to buy a kettlebell. At the same time, a good quality item is essential here. A cheap, low-value kettlebell will likely have a handle that is less superior and create the many problems we are trying to avoid. In addition, cheaper kettlebells will chip easily because they usually have paint around them and are made from inferior material as well. The plastic coverings around vinyl bells will also wear down and crack before you know it.

If you are going to purchase a kettlebell, it is best to get a cast-iron one right away. It will last you a long time and will be much more economical due to the reduced wear and tear. You will have to buy a new kettlebell far less often. A single kettlebell will run you around 50-300 dollars. Get the cheapest one you can find that still provides good value, but never sacrifice quality for the price. There is no sense in buying a kettlebell today, simply because it is cheaper, and then having to buy another one a few weeks down the line because you did not choose well the first time.

Always remember your own comfort matters. It is not worth saving a few bucks if the kettlebell you get causes injuries and just doesn't feel right to you. Consider your goals and make your decision wisely. It could save you a lot of heartaches, pain, and even money in the long run. The following are some other considerations when buying a kettlebell.

There should be some flatness at the base or very bottom of the bell section. Avoid ones with a base that is completely round, because it can make for a lot of awkwardness with certain exercises.

In addition to the outer part breaking down, kettlebells with a vinyl covering can become very slippery. Once your hand becomes slippery, the chance of major injury increases immensely. Imagine that kettlebell slipping out of your hand and landing on your foot, or hitting someone else. It won't be a pretty sight.

Do your research on reputable brands. Any good kettlebell manufacturer will provide anti-rust and anti-chip protection. This means they are confident in their brand and willing to make a guarantee. If a particular manufacturer cannot guarantee this, then they are likely to use an inferior type of material. Once again, do not skimp on the money to avoid a superior brand. Chances are, you will be paying much more on the backside and putting your safety at further risk.

How versatile do you plan on becoming? If your objective is to incorporate as many exercises as you can, then consider buying several kettlebells with different weights.

I understand that online shopping is a major platform these days. I am not knocking this. I think it's great that people can get products delivered directly to their homes, especially if they can't find them in stores. I would advise against buying kettlebells online until you really know what you are looking for. For the first time, I advise in-person shopping so you can get a good feel for it. Also, if your local gym has kettlebells, try them out and see how you like them. Remember, this is an investment so you want to make sure you are fully informed.

Once you have purchased your first kettlebell, you are ready to rock. Get ready for a workout experience you have never had before. You will be amazed at how many benefits one small piece of equipment can provide.

ADVICE ON HAND PROTECTION

If you have done weight training of any kind, you understand the risk of damaging your hands over time. It is almost inevitable to a certain degree, but there are many ways you can minimize it. Trust me my fellow men, when I tell you, that you don't have to deal with dry, cracked, painful, and callous-filled hands if you don't want to. I know, I know, it's a sign of strength, I guess. However, I would rather save my hands a little for another day.

We have already given you some advice about choosing a proper handle. Here are a few more handy (pun intended) tips for protecting your hands that you can perform every day. You will not realize how important your hands are until you are no longer able to use them. Let's avoid those gym hands, shall we? Unlike gloves, these practices will not impact your workout time or affect your results. They are simple routines you can do throughout the day.

Moisturize Daily:

Avoid doing this too close to workout time so your hands are not too slippery. There is no shame, men, in moisturizing your hands. The best times to do it are when your hands are clean, like after your shower. Moisturize twice a day with a quality lotion or moisturizer. Do this in the morning and evening before you go to bed. This practice is the best way to avoid dry, cracked hands. No matter how hard you go on that kettlebell, you will feel confident when you shake someone's hand.

Soak Your Hands Daily:

This is a great practice, whether you have gym hands already, or are trying to avoid them. It is a great way to keep hands soft. Soak your hands in warm water for about 15-20 minutes a day. You may add some Epsom salt to the water for better results. After soaking you can take what's called a pumice stone, or a filer, to slowly scratch away the rough parts of your hands. This will help get rid of any hard, excess skin, like calluses, that have developed from working out. This will keep your hands nice and smooth no matter how hard you work out and toss that kettlebell around.

Avoid Picking at Calluses:

It can be very tempting to pick at calluses and try to forcefully remove them. Men certainly love doing this. However, this will only make the situation worse for you. Each time you do this, the skin will grow back thicker and tougher. A handful of calluses can become uncomfortable, and aesthetically unpleasing. If you become way too tempted here, refer back to the first two interventions I discussed.

While men care about their appearance, they also care about looking tough. Many of these practices may not seem masculine to some, but trust me, paying attention to how you look is not unmanly. Many great men in history cared about their appearance. The legendary Frank Sinatra would get manicures regularly, and no one would dare not call him a man. Also, if you are worried about people laughing at your hands, give them a good grip that you develop during kettlebell training. The laughter will stop really quick.

A FEW OTHER CONSIDERATIONS:

As with any other workout equipment or routine, there are certain considerations you need to make. I always advise getting proper medical follow up prior to starting any new exercise routine. There may be contraindications for you using the kettlebell and this is something you need to know prior to starting. Foregoing these precautions can cause serious problems for you.

First of all, consider your medical history. Are there any medical indicators, like heart disease, or diabetes that may preclude you from using the kettlebell? Are there any joint or other musculoskeletal conditions to take into account. Seriously think about these factors before proceeding further into this book.

What was your own training background like? Are you a gym rat or more of a couch potato? Consider your fitness level before jumping into these exercises. Of course, we do start from the beginning so everyone will learn the basics first.

Finally, what type of space do you have? With the kettlebell training, you will need ample room to move around and swing that bell. If you don't have space in your home, you may have to find someplace else to go. The equipment is easy to move around so that should not be a problem. You can easily carry it anywhere. Also, consider your footwear. It is recommended to go barefoot, but if you must wear shoes, choose ones that aren't too cushioned. Weightlifting shoes over running shoes are recommended.

Chapter 4: Kettlebells Beginner's Workout

This beginner's workout is suitable for both male & female individuals who are interested in using kettlebells to improve their fitness levels either for the first time or after a very long period.

The first thing that is required when following this workout is clothing. You must be wearing lose clothing when training with kettlebells, most likely shorts or any other clothe that gives you a wide range of motion especially around the legs & arms. When it comes to footwear, kettlebell enthusiasts often tend to train barefoot which gives them full control but if you're worried about hurting yourself by stepping on uncomfortable surfaces then you can try vibram fiverfingers, which will give you both comfort and protection. Otherwise, you may train using flat-soled shoes but try to avoid fancy, uneven shoes, as you'll need to have close contact with the ground to maintain maximum balance during workouts.

The Workout:

The workout is fairly simple and will involve only two exercises namely kettlebell swings & Turkish getups. The workout will not take much of your time and require 20 minutes to complete; a two minute warm-up before the regimen is recommended in addition to one minute active recovery in between each set. Finally a 3 – 4 minute cool down session will follow after which the workout will be over. Note that your focus throughout the routine should not be to skim through the exercise at a high rate, instead you should take it slow and perform each exercise with full concentration, making sure that your posture is correct.

The exercises are explained as follows and even though some of you might not find the weights to be challenging, the exercise will become really tough as you incorporate active recovery into it.

Furthermore, starting out with light weights is essential for beginners as it's the technique that really matters in their case.

Kettlebell swings – 4 sets of 15 reps each.

Men – 16 kg.

Women – 8 kg.

The kettlebell swing is the building block of any kettlebell workout; if executed correctly, it can make up the conditions required for an intense workout, which help develop a strong posture by strengthening the glutes, back, hamstrings and shoulder muscles. Moreover, it also boosts the cardiovascular system, therefore, you should place special focus on this exercise.

The kettlebell swing will train every muscle that is required for a perfect vertical leap but instead of actually performing the leap, you transfer the force right into the kettlebell. The kettlebell will allow you to safely transfer your explosive force without tiring your entire body as sets &

reps progress. This makes the kettlebell swing an amazing exercise for improving jump levels, both broad and vertical. In addition, you will be able to sprint better and perform exercises like squats & deadlifts with maximum potential as well.

Take a wide stance to begin with and have your feet at approximately 1.5 times the width of your shoulders, with toes pointing in a slight outward direction. The stance is important, as you'll need to have space for the kettlebell when it comes swinging backwards. You'll also have more stability when the kettlebell is adjacent to the upper portion of your body.

Next, squat down without arching your back while at the same time not making it vertical; just have it in its normal stature. Lift up the weight, squat up and stand straight with your shoulders resting back. Keep your head straight while executing this step and be sure to look across the room as you do so!

Begin the movement of the kettlebell by squatting down by pushing your hips back until your groin is well clear of the kettlebell. Now flick the kettlebell back in between your legs to gain some momentum while making sure that your arms do not move during the entire process; this will be the only time when your arms will be used to manipulate the weight.

After gaining momentum, you must feel your forearms exerting a force against your groin; if this is the case then you're doing it right. The kettlebell must now be extending right behind you and as soon as it reaches its maximum decline, squat up & thrust your pelvis in the forward direction, simultaneously.

The last step will lead to a tightened back, which will result in forward propulsion of the kettlebell. You should try your best to get the kettlebell as high as your chest. If you can, then swinging it all the way to the head is also allowed but for beginners, chest height is enough of a milestone.

To keep on repeating the exercise, let the kettlebell fall into the starting position while making sure that the kettlebell is in contact with your extended arms at all times. As the bell lowers down, you'll need to squat down with it and repeat the whole process again.

Throughout the exercise you should remember that the target of the exercise is not your arms and the arms should never be used to lift the weight up. Your main focus should always remain on the glutes, back, shoulders and hamstrings.

Turkish Getups – 4 sets, 30 seconds for each set.

Men – 8 kg.

Women – 4 kg.

You must alternate the hand that holds the bell between each rep.

The Turkish Getup is a great exercise when it comes to building stronger shoulder muscles and all-round conditioning of the body. It is essential for wrestlers especially

MMA fighters, BJJ and other athletes whose main focus is combat in standing & ground positions. The whole set of movements is a freestyle one and targets the core, quads, calves and of course the shoulders. When combined with the kettlebell swing, as in the current case, it can make up for a very high intensity workout.

Begin the exercise by lying straight on the floor, facing the ceiling or sky. Grab the kettlebell and gently place it almost 12 – 15 inches beside your right arm.

Now roll onto the right side so that you face the kettlebell. Grab the kettlebell with both of your arms while they are in the bent position. Do not try to put more weight on one of the arms as this may damage that shoulder.

Roll back to the straight, lying position while making sure that you have complete grip over the kettlebell.

Slowly, let go of the kettlebell's grip from your left hand and bench press the weight of the kettlebell with your right hand. At the same time, make sure that both of the arms are making a 90 degree angle from the floor and that both the elbows are locked out. Remember to keep the kettlebell in this position unless a step guides you otherwise.

Next, bend the right knee so enough space is made for the right knee to land firmly on the ground.

Lift the right shoulder from the floor as if you're executing a twisting ab crunch; now support the weight of your body on the other elbow.

Change your position abruptly, from your elbow to your left hand but be sure to keep the hand bent out wide to avoid any damages.

Raise the butt & the extended leg off the floor and use the stability of your left hand & right leg to move your left leg closer to your body. Add balance to the movement by keeping your knee & toes in contact with the ground.

Stand up while holding the position of your kettlebell bearing arm.

Reverse the process to sit back in the starting position once again.

Even though it may seem like the exercise slow & sluggish it must always be performed in one quick movement with your eyes focused on the kettlebell.

Active Recovery:

This includes light intensity anaerobic activity like dynamic stretching, jogging, stationary bike, etc. Active recovery will help you increase the flow of blood in your body, which will result in more oxygen being delivered to muscle cells. This in turn will clean up any deposits of lactic acid that will improve muscle's recovery. The activity also has a secondary goal which is to help the heart in pumping blood; simply resting in between sets makes it a lot harder for the heart to pump blood but this particular activity will make the process smoother.

Kettlebell Beginner's Regimen:

- Warm up should be carried out with the help of stationary bikes, treadmill or skipping rope; the time limit for every warm up is 5 minutes.

- The weight guidelines for males & females must be followed.

- The warmup should be completed with 5 minutes of treadmill or jump rope.

The following program contains a full week's kettlebell workout made for beginners. The aim of the program is to make you work out 3 times a week for 6 weeks. You will be able to track your performance using the tables given below.

Fill in the weights column with the weights you used for the exercise and tick each of the reps column when they have been successfully executed. If you are only able to complete part of the exercise, then list the number of reps.

Monday's Workout

	Weight	15 reps	15 reps	15 reps	15 reps
Swing					
	Weight	30 secs	30 secs	30 secs	30 secs
Turkish getup					

Wednesday's Workout

	Weight	15 reps	15 reps	15 reps	15 reps
Swing					
	Weight	30 secs	30 secs	30 secs	30 secs
Turkish getup					

Friday's Workout

	Weight	15 reps	15 reps	15 reps	15 reps

Swing					
	Weight	30 secs	30 secs	30 secs	30 secs
Turkish getup					

Chapter 5: 30 Day Kettlebell Wod Exercises

The key to completing the 30-day kettlebell challenge is balance. You need to achieve balance in your nutrition, workout schedule and resting time. This will prevent your body from not having enough energy or from becoming injured due to over fatigue.

For beginners, it may be necessary to limit the number of workout sessions per week to three. This is to ensure that your body will have time to recover from the grueling workout. If you are already fit, you can increase frequency of sessions per week to 5. You can set one workout session a day to suit your schedule.

If you are confident that you can finish the prescribed workouts in the table below, you could try to complete it. The 30-day routine suggested below only has one rest day every 7 days. This will yield faster weight loss results. Rest is also an essential part of losing weight. Make sure that you have at least 24 hours to rest before the next workout.

The warm ups

Before each session, you should warm up the muscles that you will use first. Because we are always using the muscles in the lower and upper arms, you need to stretch them out and condition them by lifting light weight kettlebells.

Here are some warm up moves that you do to prepare your muscles for the workout ahead:

Name of Exercise	Target Muscles
Shoulder strangle	Shoulder muscles
Hand Down Spine	Shoulders and Triceps
Forearm Rotation	Elbow and lower arms
Arm Rotation	Shoulders
Standing	Quadriceps

Quadriceps Stretch

Bar Twist	Hips
Side lunge	Leg muscles

These are only some of the stretching exercises that you can use. You should choose the exercises that will stretch or warm up the muscle groups that you will use for the day.

The 30-day Workout of the Day Exercises

Day #	Kettlebell Exercise to Use	Target Muscle
1	Kettlebell Swing	Back, Shoulders, Hips, Gluteus, Legs
2	Kettlebell Power Plank with Row	Abdominal Muscles, Arms, Back
3	Kettlebell Goblet Squat	Back, Legs, Gluteus Muscles
4	Single Arm Kettlebell Floor Press	Arms, Chest, Core

5	Rest Day	
6	Kettlebell High Pull	Shoulders, Arms, Gluteus Muscles, Legs
7	Kettlebell Lunge Press	Back, Shoulders, Arms, Abdominal Muscles, Gluteus Muscles, Legs
8	Kettlebell Sumo High Pull	Back, Legs, Arms, Shoulders
9	Kettlebell Russian Twist	Abdominal Muscles, Lower Back
10	Kettlebell Windmill	Back, Shoulders, Abdominal Muscles, Oblique Muscles, hips
11	Extended Range One-arm Kettlebell Floor Press	Chest, Shoulder, Triceps
12	Rest Day	

13	Side step Kettlebell Swing	Legs, Gluteus Muscles, back
14	Kettlebell Pushup	Triceps, Chest
15	Single Arm Kettlebell Swing	Back, Shoulders, Hips, Gluteus, Legs
16	Kettlebell one-legged dead lift	Hamstrings, Gluteus Muscles, Lower Back
17	Kettlebell Pistol Squat	Quadriceps, Calves, Gluteus Muscles, Hamstrings, Shoulders
18	Leg Over Floor Press	Chest, Shoulders, Triceps
19	Rest Day	
20	Plyo Kettlebell Pushups	Chest, Shoulders, Triceps
21	Kettlebell Alternating	Back, Arms, Shoulders, Core,

	Renegade Row	Hips, Legs
22	Front Squats with two Kettlebells	Quadriceps and Gluteus Muscles
23	Kettlebell Pushup with Row	Back, Chest, Arms
24	Kettlebell Half Get up	Abdominal Muscles, Arms, Back
25	Kettlebell Figure 8	Arms, Back, Abdominal Muscles
26	Rest Day	
27	Single Arm Kettlebell Split Jerk	Back, Shoulders, Chest, Legs
28	Two-Arm Kettlebell Military Press	Back, Shoulders, Arms
29	Kettlebell clean	Butt, Legs, Back
30	Kettlebell Dead	Legs, Gluteus

| lift | Muscles, arms, back, Abdominal Muscles |

When doing the workouts above, you should do 8-10 reps using a 16kg kettlebell for men. If 16 kg is too difficult for some movements like get-ups and windmills, use a 12 kg kettlebell. Gradually work your way up the weight ladder when 10 reps is too easy for you.

Beginner women should start with 6 to 10-kilogram kettlebell. They should also start with 8 reps. Instead of increasing weights however; women who only want to lose weight should increase the number of reps.

Incorporating the Kettlebell WOD to your CrossFit Routine

After doing 8-10 reps of the Kettlebell WOD, you should follow it with 10 pushups. You should try to finish the round as fast as you can. You should do 5 rounds of this workout pair during your workout days. You could have a minute to rest in between set. You could also change the pushups to other calisthenics exercises.

To make it more challenging, you could do the same exercises on the following month. However, this time, you will record the time that you used to finish the prescribed 5 rounds. You should do the same workout on the following month while trying to lessen the time to finish the routine.

Chapter 6: Different Kettle Bell Exercises

There is no single weight category that is better than others, but it can be said that kettlebell is the most appreciated member of the free weight family. You can use kettlebells for almost anything, from high-replicated HIIT training exercises to low-replicated heavyweight to logs, and especially good for compound movements such as oscillation and squatting.

Next time you go to the gym, buy a kettle and try out some of this beginner, intermediate and advanced drills that's been selected and explained.

•Kettlebell Swing

Make your feet are slightly wider than your shoulder width. Hold the kettlebell with both hands, palms facing you, and arms in front of your body. Lower your body by gently bending your knees and pushing your hips back. Bring your hips forward and rotate the kettlebell straight at shoulder height, keeping your hip muscles and belly connected. Direct the swing down again. "

• Sumo Squat

Temp You can hold the kettlebell with both hands, holding the Templer upside down with both hands.

Your feet should be wider than shoulder-width and slightly outward. Keep your back straight, lift your chest, and hold your knee. Push your hips backward and bend your knees as you release your movements. Push your heels and push your hips forward to return to the starting position. Don't let squat roll in the ascension phase - work hard to remove your knees.

• Single Arm Kettlebell Series

Place the kettle in front of your feet, take a big step backward with your left leg and take your kettlebell in your left hand with your right arm up. "Keep your back in a stable position.

- Kettlebell Triceps Extension

Kettlebell with both hands, then bring your kettlebell back with your arms out.

Achter Figure

Kettlebell in hand on the right side of your front, you are in a dwarf or half-dwarf position (better as you go down) to make sure your back is straight and your core is hardened. Bring the kettlebell out of your right leg and then back from your legs. Grasp the kettlebell from the front with your left hand to bring your legs. To move the bell in eight steps, repeat the opposite movement.

Advanced kettlebell exercises

- Single-arm kettlebell swing

Keep your feet a little farther than the shoulder width. Hold the kettle bell handle with one hand, the palm facing you, and hold your arm in front of your body. Lower your body by gently bending your knees and pushing your hips back. Control the weight and repeat.

Kettlebell Squeeze

Rest the kettlebell on your chest and extend your arms horizontally to the floor.

• Kettlebell Goblet Squatting

Tut Hold the kettlebell upside down in both hands, the movement of the squat, is the same as a normal squat. Helps improve the squatting movement pattern while holding.

• Return of the Russian Kettlebell

Sit with your legs flat on the floor, spread the shoulder-width apart, bend your legs and lean back so that your trunk will have a 45 ° angle to the floor. Hold the kettle with both hands towards your chest.

• Single lever kettlebell flooring press

In Sit back with your legs straight, Pull the kettle into the palm of your hand and hold it over your chest.

• Wooden Train

Begin your raised board position on the floor, with your hands just below your shoulders and outstretched arms. Make sure your body draws a straight line from your shoulders to heels and that your core is hardened. Place a kettle just outside one hand.

Hold under your body, hold the kettlebell handle, and pull it to the other side. Put your hand back on the floor and repeat with the other arm. Keep your pelvis on the ground. If you start bending or bending while shooting, slow down movement, or reduce the weight of the kettle.

Advanced Kettlebell Exercises

•Single Arm Overhead Counterflow

The shoulder, so that the kettlebell rests on the forearm.

Basın Press the kettlebell at the same time. Lowering your knee over your head.

•Peasant Walk

Take something with the heavy kettlebells, keep them with you and go as far as you can.

- Kettlebell Pressing Series

Starting in the printing position spread your hand's shoulder wide and holds the kettlebell handles with your feet. Apply pressure and then place a row on the top of the print, lift the right elbow, and squeeze the shoulder blades so that your elbow crosses your body. Lower it with your left hand and continue rowing with your left hand. Then press repeatedly to continue the next repeat.

- "Kettlebell Cleaning and Compression

Take a kettle while standing on the floor and pull the kettlebell towards your shoulder and shake the kettlebell over your wrist. Then walk along with the heels and explode your knees and hips to create momentum. While doing this, push the kettlebell over your head until your arm is fully extended.

- One-Kettlebell Squat Stool

Ley Clean the kettlebell and squeeze it with one arm, so you can stand upright while holding your arm above your head, or he says. If you look straight ahead and hold your arm out, bend your knees and lower your upper body and push your hips back to keep your chin and chest up. When your thighs are parallel to the floor, spread your heels, and stretch your legs and hips so that you can return to the starting position.

•Angel Press

If you want to work on your kernel and feel burns on your body's shoulders, the name of this exercise is yours.

Use a kettle with a weight that you can easily push upwards. Sit on the floor with your knees bent and hold both arms with outstretched arms and a back. Lower the upholstery in a controlled manner and position the kettlebells towards your chest: the slower, the better the burn.

Then, squeeze your abdominal muscles and put your upper body upright, with your arms on your head with your head spinning.

Chapter 7: Exercise Toolkit

In addition to the earlier described and illustrated three key moves of the kettlebell swing, kettlebell Turkish getup and kettlebell squat press, below are additional mixes of excellent compound moves to add to your toolkit. Each move is designed to engage the most muscles possible in the most fluid, functional way.

Compound Moves to Target Your Back

Renegade Row

Great for stabilising the core.

Great compound move in that you exercise multiple large muscle groups in one large move.

Improves balance when done on two kettlebells.

The addition of push-ups in the movement makes for a great chest and back exercise.

Aim for 20 x reps and 3 x sets

Place two kettlebells on the ground about shoulder width apart.

In a push up position, place your hands on the grip section of each Kettlebell for support.

Place your legs to slightly wider than hip width apart with your toes supporting your weight. This is the start position.

Push down through one kettlebell and at the same time "row" the opposite one upwards by retracting your shoulder and bending your elbow.

Lower the kettlebell to the floor and without pause, then repeat the movement with your other arm.

When you have rowed both arms that is one repetition.

Single arm Kettlebell pulls

Great for developing a strong back and core.

Always keep a straight back to avoid putting any unnecessary strain on your lower back.

Ensure you pull your shoulder right back to get the most out of the exercise.

Aim for 20 x reps, 10 per arm and 3 x sets

Place a kettlebell in front of you

Place your right leg forward and rest your left leg on the ball of your left foot (similar to a lunge stance.)

Bend your knees slightly as you bend over to get in the starting position.

Keep your back straight.

Rest your right hand on your right knee for stability.

Grip the kettlebell with a neutral grip in your left hand.

Pull the kettlebell up to your stomach, retracting your shoulder blade and flexing your elbow. Keep your back straight. Lower and repeat.

Complete all the repetitions for one side before switching.

Pull-ups

Classic move which can be varied from close grip to wide grip to work different parts of the back

Always tense up your core while performing pull-ups as it will help you recruit further muscles to aid in the movement.

A towel can be hung over the bar and used to preform pull-ups to increase grip strength.

Knees can be raised during the pull-up motion to work the abdominals.

Aim for 20reps, although if you are a beginner using a machine or band to build up your reps is advisable.

Standing under a pull up bar, reach up and hold onto the bar with an overhand grip. Keep your arms straight and hang from the bar so that your arms are taking all of your weight.

Keeping your body straight and not swinging your weight, pull your body up towards the bar by pulling your elbows down towards your torso at an angle.

Continue lifting until your chest is nearly touching the bar. You should feel a "squeeze" at the base of your lats (about midway down your back and to the side) as they contract.

Once your lats have completely contracted at the top of the movement, slowly lower your body to the starting position.

Suspension Strap Row

Once you begin to find reps to easy consider putting feet on a swiss ball to increase difficulty and engage your core.

Ensure you pull your shoulders right back to get the most out of the move.

Aim for 30 reps and 3 sets.

Grip the suspension straps. Stand facing the straps, brace your lower back and your core.

Lean back, letting the straps hold your weight. Your arms should be straight.

Pull yourself up with your back, maintaining a tight core.

Squeeze the back muscles and slowly lower yourself. Repeat.

If looking for additional difficulty then place a swissball in front of yourself and rest your heels on the top of it. Now raise yourself up to the point where you find balance before preforming steps 1-4.

Chapter 8: Mistakes To Avoid

People who are new at an exercise regimen should take time to learn proper technique and avoid mistakes. It is easy to acquire injury if you are practicing incorrectly.

Not following proper movement progression

People may be tempted to try out exercises that are too advanced for their fitness level. This can easily result to back injury. For example, beginners should always master the dead lifts first before the swing.

How to avoid:

Avoid this mistake by training slowly. You can watch videos to see how the movement is done.

Not maintaining neutral spine

Keeping your neck in neutral spine ensures that your body is in correct alignment. You should keep this in mind while performing intermediate kettlebell exercises such as high pulls, swing and clean. When your body is not correctly aligned, your entire spine and the muscles around it may acquire injury.

How to avoid:

Remember to keep your hips and head in a straight line. Keep your back straight.

Too wide stance

Almost every kettlebell exercises require you to keep your feet apart. However, taking stance that is too wide can make you vulnerable to injury. Area of risk includes hips, knees and lower back.

How to avoid:

Remember to take an athletic stance. It is where your legs are hip wide apart and would make it easy for you to jump.

Muscling the bell with the upper body

Avoid over emphasizing the muscles in the upper body because this deteriorates the exercise flow and can place strain in your body. You may experience neck, shoulders and lower back injury if you focus too much on your upper body.

How to avoid:

Make sure to relax your upper body and lock out the knees with every repetition.

Training until muscles fail

It is important to challenge yourself with every repetition but you should never experience extreme pain while working out. Whenever you push yourself too much, you will be vulnerable to injury and muscle fatigue.

How to avoid:

Take a rest after several repetitions.

Attempting to rescue a bad repetition

Always pay attention to your movements. If something does not feel right, stop and check your posture or how you hold the kettlebell before resuming the exercise.

How to avoid:

Never try to force bad repetitions. Always be conscious of your form while exercising.

Try anything fancy

Trying to invent fancy moves that are different from the basic movements of exercise can be very risky. Your body might not be prepared for the exercise and can result to spine injury. Many things can go wrong if you try to do spontaneous and wacky movements with a kettlebell.

How to avoid:

Try to stick to the basic movements as much as possible because they tend to work the best. Incorporate the basic principles of kettlebell exercise even if you do try more challenging moves.

Using a tight grip

Gripping the handle too tight is pointless and can be dangerous. You can be vulnerable to hand and elbow injuries.

How to avoid:

Relax your hands and hold the handle with your fingers rather than the palms.

Smashing the forearms

Some kettlebell exercise movements like the clean and snatch changes the position of the bell during the movement. You should control the bell so that it does not fall and smash your arms.

How to avoid:

Thrust the kettlebell upwards instead of swinging it overhead. Gently relax your grip to allow the kettlebell to rest into your forearm.

Wearing improper footwear

Improper footwear does not only include slippers and open toe sandals. Running shoes are also not advisable for kettlebell trainings because it can raise the heel and push the knee forward during squats which can result to knee injury.

How to avoid:

Try to train in flat soled shoes.

Chapter 9: Kettlebell Slingshot

This is a exercise is great fun and really gets the heart beating but it is effective at building muscle too.

Muscle Targeted: Arms, Back, Abs and Obliques

Method:

Keep your feet a shoulder width apart and pick up the kettlebell with one hand. Let the kettlebell hang in front of you. Swing the kettlebell to your side and then around behind your back. Move your arm that is not holding the kettlebelll to the other side of your back and pass the kettlebell from one hand to the other. Bring the kettlebell back out from behind your back on the other side and move it around to the front. Take the kettlebell in the other hand (the hand it started in) and repeat the movement back around and then around. After 10 reps, switch directions.

Video: https://www.youtube.com/watch?v=wrbjfSdKs4s

Top Tips:

-While you should aim to use the swinging motion to your advantage, don't make the movement erratic or rely on the momentum. Aim for control.

-Start with a lighter weight to begin with, until you get the hang of the passing over behind the back.

Kettlebell Snatch

The Kettlebell snatch is another classic lift that works great with kettlebells. It is explosive and really gets your heart pumping.

Muscles Targeted: Chest, Back, and Shoulders

Method:

Start with your feet a shoulder width apart and a kettlebell between them. Bend your knees and maintain a loose posture, using the natural spring in your legs. Bend and take the handle of the kettlebell in one hand. Breathe in and explode upwards. Feel the movement starting from your toes and visualize the weight coming up in a straight line perpendicular to the floor. Pull the kettlebell upwards until it reaches the chest level and then flip your elbow out underneath it and continue the single upwards motion. This is one movement and you should not stop and press at anytime. Once the weight is overhead, hold the position for a moment before returning the weight to the starting position and continuing with your set. After the set, switch arms.

Video: https://www.youtube.com/watch?v=6MGUllzX_0g

Top Tips:

- Remember, this is one continuous movement.

- The more explosive you can be at the bottom of the rep, the easier it will be at the top of the rep.

- When the kettlebell is overhead, keep your core tight to stabilize yourself.

Two arm kettlebell military press

The two-arm kettlebell military press may be one of the best exercises to build big shoulders. It should aim to be coordinated and controlled.

Muscles targeted: Arms, Shoulders and Back

Method:

Take two kettlebells and grab one in each hand. 'Clean' them up into the 'rack' or 'racking' position. In a controlled and coordinated motion, press the kettlebells up from the chest above your head. Aim to have your arms moving at the same pace so the weights are positioned at a similar level. At the top of the rep, lean forward at the waist so that the weights up positioned up behind the head. Hold momentarily and then bring them back down to the starting 'rack' position. Continue this pressing movement in a smooth manner until you finish your set.

Video: https://www.youtube.com/watch?v=iW-PGDQwmn8

Top Tips:

-It is really important to keep the two kettlebells at an equal level; this will help you stay balanced.

-Keep your core tight to also help stabilize.

-Focus on your breathing; this will help you with the rhythm of the movement.

-Don't be tempted to cheat by bouncing up on your knees to help with the pressing motion!

Single arm Kettlebell row

The single arm kettlebell row is great for working the back and shoulders. It relies on a straight back and tight core.

Muscles Targeted: Arms, Back and Shoulders

Method:

Stand a shoulder width apart and place a kettlebell between your legs. Bend at the knees slightly, keeping your black flat and your neck in a neutral position. Grab the kettlebell so that your knuckles are facing outwards. Pull the kettlebells up towards your stomach. You shouldn't aim to stand up, move your knees or back. This is a row, so the movement should be as if on a rowing machine, with your elbows moving backwards. The movement should be fluid. Keep your elbow close to your body. At the top of the rep tense your core and keep everything tight, then slowly drop the weights in a controlled motion back towards the starting position. Repeat.

Video: https://www.youtube.com/watch?v=J3zfFc1UfHo

Top tips:

-Don't crane your neck upwards; aim to keep your neck in a neutral position.

-Visualize the movement while doing it. It should be fluid and piston like.

Chapter 10: Foundational Movement Cues And Terms

I have links to videos of all of the movements listed in this guide at www.jvictorfitness.com, and I encourage you to visit the site to see live demos. However, I will offer some foundational cues that you should be conscious of when performing kettlebell movements.

The swing

The swing is the foundational movement for kettlebell training - almost every other movement uses the same type of momentum that you create with the kettlebell swing. The swing is also one of the best full-body functional movements.

Start with an appropriate weight on the floor. With legs a little more than shoulder width apart, hold the kettlebell by the handle and pull up to the legs. Initiate the swing by moving the hips and swinging the kettlebell to your shoulders. Once you build momentum, keep a consistent hip-hinge and explode to move the kettlebell with swinging momentum.

There are two basic types of swings to mention. The Russian swing finishes at shoulder level, whereas the American swing finishes overhead. In this guide, I will just write "kettlebell swing" but experiment with the two to see which works best in a workout. The American swing is generally done with less weight but for more reps and can activate the core more, whereas the Russian swing will use more weight for less overall reps, but will increase strength to a higher degree.

Clean

The clean is when you take the kettlebell from a swing and transition into the front rack position. The end position is holding the kettlebell in a stable position in the triangle shape of your arm. The clean is a movement that can be performed by itself with heavy weight and reps, or it can be linked together with other movements such as a squat or press.

Snatch

A snatch is similar to a clean, but instead of ending the front rack position you end with the kettlebell overhead. Begin with a single-hand swing and explosively (power) throw your arm above your head, catching the kettlebell behind your head and over your head. This is the end of the movement.

You will find that you are able to do less weight with a snatch than with a clean, as the power requirements are larger. However, you can still link it with other movements like an overhead squat or lunge.

Get-up

The get-up is one of the foundational and most functional movements in athletic training. It involves starting in a laying position, gripping the kettlebell on your shoulder, pressing the kettlebell above your chest and transitioning to standing with the kettlebell overhead.

The get-up is one of the best movements around and I highly recommend watching videos before attempting it as it is very complex and difficult to break down without seeing it in real time.

Hike

Hiking the kettlebell means taking the kettlebell from the ground into a swing and into the final position. To begin a hike, the kettlebell will be a little further in front of you and between your legs on the ground, you will pull the kettlebell back to initiate the swing and then transition into the final, front rack position. A hike to clean, for example, would involve starting the ground, pulling into a swing and ending the front rack position.

Front rack

The front rack position is the resting position in the clean or lunge. The front rack position is when you have full-body stability and are holding the kettlebell handles while the horns go to the sides of the wrists and the bell rests in the triangle of your arms and in front of your shoulders.

Chapter 11: 30 Days Program

The core advantage of a kettlebell training is that it does not require a wide range of weight increments to create a workout with them as compared to dumbbells. This is mainly due to its unique shape, which allows doing multiple exercises depending on the requirement of the body. If kettlebells are included in, the workout then proves to be beneficial as it helps to build strength and burn fat. Moreover, develop the requisite stability and mobility to graduate to more advanced exercises

This year we have introduced kettlebell training, which is broken down into five weeks for beginners. During this course of the period, the aim of the challenge is to build muscles with right exercises that will help to improve athleticism and prevent injuries in the back, shoulders, hips, knees, etc. This will also clean up movement patterns so that all the challengers can perform more efficiently. The first week will focus on upper body, lower body, core, or cardio and later the challenge will target high-intensity workout, which will enable to perform two supersets with 10 moves each. All this together will develop more stability and flexibility in the body and fix asymmetries.

How to use the table?

Here is the list of the exercises and its abbreviations:

Exercises	Abbreviation
Russian Kettlebell Swing	RS
Kettlebell Figure-8	F8
Kettlebell Goblet Squat	GS
Kettlebell High Pull	HP
Kettlebell Clean	KC
Single-Arm Kettlebell Split Jerk	SJ
Two-Arm Kettlebell Military Press	MP

Kettlebell Push-Up with Row   KP

Kettlebell Windmill   WM

Side Step Kettlebell Swing: SS

Each day you will be assigned to do 2 exercises. I will tell you how many reps you should do or how long you should do the exercise. If the exercise is too easy for you, increase the weight. So, enjoy your workout. I hope you have fun and get the result you desire.

Week 1

Day1

RS	**F8**
x12-15 reps -	2 min - rest 1 min
rest 1 min	2 min - rest 1 min
x12-15 reps -	2 min - rest 1 min
rest 1 min	
x12-15 reps -	
rest 1 min	

Day2

F8	**SJ**
2 min - rest 1 min	4-6 reps per arm - rest 1 min
2 min - rest 1 min	4-6 reps per arm - rest 1 min
2 min - rest 1 min	4-6 reps per arm - rest 1 min

Day3

SS	**F8**
10-15 reps each - rest 1 min	2 min - rest 1 min
10-15 reps each - rest 1 min	2 min - rest 1 min
10-15 reps each - rest 1 min	2 min - rest 1 min

Day4

SJ	**MP**
4-6 reps per arm - rest 1 min	10-20 reps - rest 1 min
4-6 reps per arm - rest 1 min	10-20 reps - rest 1 min
4-6 reps per arm - rest 1 min	10-20 reps - rest 1 min

Day5

KC   **F8**

10-15 reps - 2 min - rest 1 min
rest 1 min 2 min - rest 1 min
10-15 reps - 2 min - rest 1 min
rest 1 min
10-15 reps -
rest 1 min

Day6

KC   **HP**

x10-15 reps - 10-12 reps - rest 1 min
rest 1 min
x10-15 reps - 10-12 reps - rest 1 min
rest 1 min
x10-15 reps - 10-12 reps - rest 1 min
rest 1 min

Day7

Rest

Week 2

Day8

KP   **SJ**

5-8 reps - rest 1   4-6 reps per arm

min	- rest 1 min
5-8 reps - rest 1 min	4-6 reps per arm - rest 1 min
5-8 reps - rest 1 min	4-6 reps per arm - rest 1 min

Day9

RS	F8
x12-15 reps - rest 1 min	2 min - rest 1 min
x12-15 reps - rest 1 min	2 min - rest 1 min
x12-15 reps - rest 1 min	2 min - rest 1 min

Day10

MP	KP
10-20 reps - rest 1 min	5-8 reps - rest 1 min
10-20 reps - rest 1 min	5-8 reps - rest 1 min
10-20 reps - rest 1 min	5-8 reps - rest 1 min

Day11

SJ **MP**

4-6 reps per arm - rest 1 min   10-20 reps - rest 1 min
4-6 reps per arm - rest 1 min   10-20 reps - rest 1 min
4-6 reps per arm - rest 1 min   10-20 reps - rest 1 min

Day12

SS   **WM**

10-15 reps each - rest 1 min   2 min - rest 1 min
10-15 reps each - rest 1 min   2 min - rest 1 min
10-15 reps each - rest 1 min   2 min - rest 1 min

Day13

GS   **WM**

15-20 reps - rest 1 min   2 min - rest 1 min
15-20 reps - rest 1 min   2 min - rest 1 min
15-20 reps - rest 1 min   2 min - rest 1 min

Day14

Rest

Week 3

Day 15

SS	KC
10-15 reps - rest 1 min	10-15 reps - rest 1 min
10-15 reps - rest 1 min	10-15 reps - rest 1 min
10-15 reps - rest 1 min	10-15 reps - rest 1 min

Day 16

KP	WM
5-8 reps - rest 1 min	2 min - rest 1 min
5-8 reps - rest 1 min	2 min - rest 1 min
5-8 reps - rest 1 min	2 min - rest 1 min

Day 17

SJ	GS
4-6 reps - rest 1 min per arm	15-20 reps - rest 1 min
4-6 reps - rest 1	15-20 reps - rest

min per arm	1 min
4-6 reps - rest 1 min per arm	15-20 reps - rest 1 min

Day18

KC	HP
10-15 reps - rest 1 min	10-12 reps - rest 1 min
10-15 reps - rest 1 min	10-12 reps - rest 1 min
10-15 reps - rest 1 min	10-12 reps - rest 1 min

Day19

SS	GS
10-15 reps - rest 1 min	15-20 reps - rest 1 min
10-15 reps - rest 1 min	15-20 reps - rest 1 min
10-15 reps - rest 1 min	15-20 reps - rest 1 min

Day20

KP	RS
5-8 reps - rest 1 min	12-15 reps - rest 1 min

| 5-8 reps - rest 1 min | 12-15 reps - rest 1 min |
| 5-8 reps - rest 1 min | 12-15 reps - rest 1 min |

Day21

Rest

Week 4

Day22

HP	SS
10-12 reps - rest 1 min	10-15 reps - rest 1 min
10-12 reps - rest 1 min	10-15 reps - rest 1 min
10-12 reps - rest 1 min	10-15 reps - rest 1 min

Day23

MP	SS
10-20 reps - rest 1 min	10-15 reps - rest 1 min
10-20 reps - rest 1 min	10-15 reps - rest 1 min

10-20 reps - rest 1 min | 10-15 reps - rest 1 min

Day24

WM
20 reps - rest 1 min
20 reps - rest 1 min
20 reps - rest 1 min

F8
2 min - rest 1 min
2 min - rest 1 min
2 min - rest 1 min

Day25

RS
12-15 reps - rest 1 min
12-15 reps - rest 1 min
12-15 reps - rest 1 min

F8
2 min - rest 1 min
2 min - rest 1 min
2 min - rest 1 min

Day26

WM
20 reps - rest 1 min
20 reps - rest 1 min

RS
12-15 reps - rest 1 min
12-15 reps - rest

min | 1 min
20 reps - rest 1 min | 12-15 reps - rest 1 min

Day27

SJ
4-6 reps per arm - rest 1 min
4-6 reps per arm - rest 1 min
4-6 reps per arm - rest 1 min

F8
2 min - rest 1 min
2 min - rest 1 min
2 min - rest 1 min

Day28

Rest

Week5

Day29

GS
15-20 reps - rest 1 min
15-20 reps - rest 1 min

SJ
4-6 reps - rest 1 min per arm
4-6 reps - rest 1 min per arm

15-20 reps - rest 1 min | 4-6 reps - rest 1 min per arm

Day30

SS | WM
10-15 reps - rest 1 min each | 2 min - rest 1 min
10-15 reps - rest 1 min each | 2 min - rest 1 min
10-15 reps - rest 1 min each | 2 min - rest 1 min

Day31

HP | WM
10-12 reps - rest 1 min | 2 min - rest 1 min
10-12 reps - rest 1 min | 2 min - rest 1 min
10-12 reps - rest 1 min | 2 min - rest 1 min

Day32

KC | MP
10-15 reps - rest 1 min | 10-20 reps - rest 1 min
10-15 reps - | 10-20 reps - rest

| rest 1 min | 1 min |
| 10-15 reps - rest 1 min | 10-20 reps - rest 1 min |

Day33

RS	F8
12-15 reps - rest 1 min	2 min - rest 1 min
12-15 reps - rest 1 min	2 min - rest 1 min
12-15 reps - rest 1 min	2 min - rest 1 min

Day34

WM	KP
20 reps - rest 1 min	5-8 reps - rest 1 min
20 reps - rest 1 min	5-8 reps - rest 1 min
20 reps - rest 1 min	5-8 reps - rest 1 min

Day35

Rest

Chapter 12: Intermediate Kettlebell Workouts

In this chapter, I will be taking your upper body, core, and lower body kettlebell workouts to the next level by providing you with intermediate workouts.

Before you perform any of the workouts in the intermediate chapter, practice the exercises without your kettlebell. Be mindful of how your body moves through the exercise and of any weaknesses or instabilities that present themselves. Develop good form without the added weight before you bring your kettlebell into the workout. Good form is crucial to getting the most out of your workout and preventing injury.

Tip: It is always a good idea to consider booking a session or two with a kettlebell instructor to help you master your form. A professional can view your movement in an objective manner from various angles, providing guidance to ensure that you are performing each movement in an exercise properly.

Important note: Many exercises throughout the workouts refer to placing your kettlebell in a racked position. Please refer to the explanation and image in Chapter 5 for beginners.

Lunges and Squats: If you have trouble knees and experience difficulty with performing squats or lunges, only take the exercise as far as you can comfortably. As you build your strength, you can try dipping lower. If you aren't able to do a full squat or lunge, just keep performing the exercise at a comfortable level for your joints.

When to increase weight or reps: Please refer to Chapter 8 for guidelines on when to increase your kettlebell weight or repetitions and sets.

INTERMEDIATE UPPER BODY KETTLEBELL WORKOUT

Shoulder salutation	8 - 10	3 - 5
Clean and press	8 - 10	3 - 5
Overhead squat	8 - 10	3 - 5
Burpee pull up	8 - 10	3 - 5
Single-handed dead lift	8 - 10	3 - 5

Rest period between sets: 30 seconds to two minutes, decrease the rest time as you progress and get fitter.

SHOULDER SALUTATION

Muscles targeted: Shoulders, back, core, quads, hamstrings

Stand with your knees bent and your torso hinged forward from the hips at a 45-degree angle to the ground.

Grip your kettlebell on either side of the body and hold it in front of you with your arms extended at shoulder height. Your arms should be parallel to the ground.

Bend your knees further into a semi-squat position and at the same time raise your arms until they are at the same 45-degree angle as your torso.

Keep your back straight throughout this exercise.

Return to the starting position with your knees slightly bent and arms extended parallel to the ground.

CLEAN AND PRESS

Muscles targeted: Shoulders, back, core, quads, glutes, hamstrings

Stand with your feet shoulder-width apart, holding your kettlebell in the racked position. This is the same position that you will finish your repetition in.

Extend your elbow and swing your kettlebell in a downward arc. As it is swinging downward, bend your knees and hinge your torso forward from your hips, allowing your kettlebell to swing between your legs.

As your kettlebell swings forward again, straighten your legs and torso back into a standing position. While straightening up, thrust your hips forward, the power from your hip thrust will add momentum to your kettlebell's upward swing.

As your kettlebell swings upwards, bend your elbow and bring it back into the racked position.

From the racked position, extend your arm straight overhead to perform a press. Ensure that your arm is straight with your wrist, elbow, and shoulder in line with each other.

Return to the racked position.

Variation: Clean and Push Press

Give your clean and press that little bit extra by adding a half squat. Perform your clean which will bring your kettlebell into the racked position. Before you perform the press, do a half squat. As you push up from the half squat to a standing position, use the momentum to extend your arm into the press.

OVERHEAD SQUAT

Muscles targeted: shoulders, core, glutes, hamstrings, quads

Stand with your feet shoulder-width apart, holding your kettlebell in the racked position.

From the racked position, extend your arm straight overhead to perform a press. Ensure that your arm is straight with your wrist, elbow, and shoulder in line with each other.

Bend your knees and hinge your torso forward from the hips to perform a squat. Keep your back straight.

Return to a standing position.

BURPEE PULL UP

Muscles targeted: core, shoulders, back, glutes, hamstrings

Stand in a relaxed, neutral position; feet shoulder-width apart, with your kettlebell between your feet.

Bend your knees and hinge your torso forward from the hips to perform a squat.

Place your hands shoulder-width apart on either side of your kettlebell.

Keep your arms straight.

In a swift, fluid motion jump both feet backward. You should now be in a push up or plank pose.

Perform one push up.

Jump both feet forward so that you are in a squatting position again with your hands on either side of your kettlebell.

Grip the top of your kettlebell handle with both hands.

Return to a standing position, lifting your kettlebell with you.

Do not stop your kettlebell's momentum. Bend your elbows and bring the kettlebell up to your chest. Make sure that your elbows are out to the side and parallel to the ground.

Lower your kettlebell to thigh height.

Squat down and place your kettlebell on the ground between your feet.

Variations:

Burpee Clean: Replace your pull up with a kettlebell clean by altering the exercise as follows:

Jump both feet forward so that you are in a squatting position again with your hands on either side of your kettlebell.

Grip the top of your kettlebell handle with one hand.

While straightening up, thrust your hips forward, the power from your hip thrust will add momentum to your kettlebell's upward swing.

As your kettlebell swings upwards, bend your elbow and bring it into the racked position.

Extend your elbow and swing your kettlebell in a downward arc. As it is swinging downward, bend your knees and hinge your torso forward from your hips to place your kettlebell back on the ground between your feet.

Burpee Press: Swap the pull up and perform a press instead, here's how to substitute the move:

Jump both feet forward so that you are in a squatting position again with your hands on either side of your kettlebell.

Grip the top of your kettlebell handle with one hand.

While straightening up, thrust your hips forward, the power from your hip thrust will add momentum to your kettlebell's upward swing.

As your kettlebell swings upwards, bend your elbow and bring it into the racked position.

From the racked position, extend your arm straight overhead to perform a press.

Ensure that your arm is straight with your wrist, elbow, and shoulder in line with each other.

Return to the racked position.

Extend your elbow and swing your kettlebell in a downward arc. As it is swinging downward, bend your knees and hinge your torso forward from your hips to place your kettlebell back on the ground between your feet.

SINGLE-HANDED DEADLIFT

Muscles targeted: shoulders, back, core, glutes, hamstrings, quads

Stand in a relaxed, neutral position; feet shoulder-width apart, with your kettlebell between your feet.

Bend your knees and hinge your torso forward from the hips. Keep your back straight.

Grip your kettlebell firmly by the handle with one hand.

Straighten up to a standing position, lifting your kettlebell with you. Your kettlebell should be hanging in front of your body at thigh level.

Bend your knees and hinge your torso forward from the hips to place your kettlebell back on the ground between your feet.

Be sure to keep your shoulders straight and level.

INTERMEDIATE CORE KETTLEBELL WORKOUT

Sit up and press	8 - 10	3 - 5
Renegade row	8 - 10 per side	3 - 5
Russian twist	8 - 10 per side	3 - 5
Mountain climbers	45 - 60 seconds	3 - 5

| Lateral bend | 8 - 10 per side | 3 - 5 |

Rest period between sets: 30 seconds to two minutes, decrease the rest time as you progress, and get fitter.

SIT UP AND PRESS

Muscles targeted: core, back, shoulders

Sit on the floor. Your legs should either be straight in front of you or bent at the knee, similar to the position for regular sit-ups.

Grip your kettlebell on either side of the handle and bring it to your chest.

Lie back on the floor, holding your kettlebell to your chest.

Perform a regular sit up while holding your kettlebell lightly against your chest. Don't push it out forward or let it sink into your lap.

Once in a sitting position, raise your kettlebell overhead to perform a two-handed press and then lower your kettlebell back to your chest.

Lower yourself back onto the floor.

Be sure to engage your core muscles to perform the sit up and not your lower back to prevent injury.

Variation: Straight Arm Sit Up

Up the ante of this exercise by gripping your kettlebell in one hand while lying back on the floor. Straighten your arm to raise your kettlebell overhead. Perform the sit up while holding your kettlebell overhead, keeping your arm pointing straight at the ceiling.

RENEGADE ROW

Muscles targeted: core, shoulders, back, glutes, hamstrings, quads

For this exercise, you will need your kettlebell and an object that is roughly the same height as the top of your kettlebell handle. You can use a wooden box, for example.

Place your wooden box, or another support item, and your kettlebell shoulder-width apart on the floor.

Assume a plank or push up position with one hand on top of your support and the other gripping the top of your kettlebell handle.

Raise your kettlebell off the floor by bending your elbow and pulling back towards the ceiling.

Lower your kettlebell by extending your arm down towards the floor. Do not fully extend your arm or put your kettlebell back on the floor, keep it about an inch off the ground.

RUSSIAN TWIST

Muscles targeted: core, back, shoulders

Sit on the floor with your knees bent.

Grip your kettlebell on either side of the handle and bring it to your chest.

Lean back at a 45-degree angle.

Twist your torso to the left, bringing your kettlebell across your lap to your left side.

Lower your kettlebell as if to put it down on your left but stop about an inch above the ground.

Twist your torso to the right, bringing your kettlebell across your lap to your right side.

Lower your kettlebell as if to put it down on your right but stop about an inch above the ground.

MOUNTAIN CLIMBERS

Muscles targeted: core, shoulders, back, hamstrings, quads, glutes

Assume a plank or push up position with your kettlebell placed beneath your chest and your arms straight, both hands side-by-side gripping the handle firmly. Your kettlebell should be exactly beneath your chest and shoulders so that your wrist, elbow, and shoulder are in line with each other directly over the handle of your kettlebell.

You will know that the placement of your kettlebell is correct when it doesn't wobble or threaten to fall over under you. If it wobbles and you cannot maintain the position, your kettlebell may be too far forward. When your arms are straight and your elbows locked, there should be a perfectly straight line from your shoulder to your wrist and the kettlebell handle.

Once you have gotten into position comfortably, bring one knee up towards your chest, placing all your weight on the other leg and your arms.

Extend your leg back into place and repeat with the other leg.

The aim of this exercise is to mimic a high-knee running action in the plank position to really work your core muscles.

LATERAL BEND

Muscles targeted: core, shoulders, back

Stand with your feet shoulder-width apart, your kettlebell gripped firmly in your right hand and hanging at your side.

Lean your weight into your left hip and bend to your right as far as you can comfortably.

Hold the position for a count of one before straightening up.

INTERMEDIATE LOWER BODY KETTLEBELL WORKOUT

Single-handed kettlebell swing	8 - 10 per side	3 - 5
Racked squat and press	8 - 10 per side	3 - 5
Racked lunge and press	8 - 10 per side	3 - 5
Sumo square with front and back jumps	8 - 10	3 - 5
Overhead double lunge	8 - 10	3 - 5

Rest period between sets: 30 seconds to two minutes, decrease the rest time as you progress, and get fitter.

SINGLE-HANDED KETTLEBELL SWING

Muscles targeted: quads, glutes, hamstrings, shoulders, core, back

Stand with your feet shoulder-width apart, knees slightly bent, and torso hinged forward from the hips. Keep your back straight while your torso is hinged forward.

Grip the top of your kettlebell handle with one hand.

Lift your kettlebell off the ground and allow it to swing back between your legs.

Straighten up to a standing position, thrusting your hips forward. The hip thrust will offer momentum to your kettlebell swing.

Swing your kettlebell out in front of you in an arch until it reaches chest height while keeping your arm straight.

As your kettlebell swings downward again, bend your knees and hinge your torso forward from the hips and allow the kettlebell to swing between your legs.

RACKED SQUAT AND PRESS

Muscles targeted: glutes, hamstrings, quads, shoulders, back, core

Stand with your feet shoulder-width apart, holding your kettlebell in the racked position.

Bend your knees and hinge your torso forward from the hips to perform a squat.

Return to a standing position.

From the racked position, extend your arm straight overhead to perform a press. Ensure that your arm is straight with your wrist, elbow, and shoulder in line with each other.

Lower your kettlebell back into the racked position.

Variation: Double Kettlebell Racked Squat and Press

If you have two kettlebells of the same weight, you can make this exercise a little bit more difficult by using both bells, one in each hand, in the racked position to add extra resistance weight.

RACKED LUNGE AND PRESS

Muscles targeted: glutes, hamstrings, quads, shoulders, back, core

Stand with your feet shoulder-width apart, holding your kettlebell in the racked position.

Step into a lunge position by either stepping back into a reverse lunge or forward into a regular lunge.

As you perform the lunge, extend your arm straight overhead to perform a press. Ensure that your arm is straight with your wrist, elbow, and shoulder in line with each other.

Return to a standing position, returning your kettlebell to the racked position as you do so.

When performing the lunge, the side you are holding the kettlebell should be the same side as your forward-facing knee.

Tip: If performing the press and lunge simultaneously is too challenging, perform the lunge and hold the position while performing the press. Bring your kettlebell back to the racked hold before returning to a standing position.

SUMO SQUAT WITH FRONT AND BACK JUMP

Muscles targeted: glutes, hamstrings, quads, back, core

Stand in a relaxed, neutral position; feet wider than shoulder-width apart, with your kettlebell between your feet.

Bend your knees and hinge forward from the hips to perform a wide squat until your thighs are parallel to the ground. Keep your back straight.

Grip your kettlebell firmly by the handle with both hands.

Return to a standing position, lifting your kettlebell with you and letting it hang down in front of you.

Repeat the wide squat to place your kettlebell back on the ground.

From the squat position, push off the ground in an explosive backward jump away from your kettlebell.

Land with your knees slightly bent and resume the wide squat.

Push off the ground again in an explosive forward jump back toward your kettlebell and return to a standing position.

OVERHEAD DOUBLE LUNGE

Muscles targeted: shoulders, core, hamstrings, glutes, quads

Stand with your feet shoulder-width apart, holding your kettlebell in the racked position.

Extend your arm straight overhead to perform a press. Ensure that your arm is straight with your wrist, elbow, and shoulder in line with each other.

Step backward with your left leg in a reverse lunge.

Return to a standing position.

Step forward with your left leg in a regular lunge.

Return to a standing position.

When performing the lunge, the side you are holding the kettlebell should be the same side as your forward-facing knee.

Conclusion

Indeed, kettlebells have come a very long way from the time when they used as muscle-building tools for strongmen in Russia. Today, they are used as fitness tools by both men and women around the world. They are no longer just for building strength, but also endurance, power, and weight loss. Therefore, instead of investing lots of money buying a treadmill, you can choose to lose weight with simple kettlebells that are quite inexpensive.

One thing that is important to note is that training with kettlebells is very advantageous. Not only you will be able to reach your fitness goals, but also learn how to adopt a healthier lifestyle.

If you are looking for a fitness workout that is challenging enough and has a proven track record of benefits, then kettlebell training is the type of workout you have been looking for! They are not only inherently strength-based but also have the ability to challenge the muscles because all you are doing is lifting

weights but working a wide range of major muscles across the body. The more weight you add, the stronger you become.

The good news with kettlebells is that you can use them for cardio too. Most kettlebell exercises involve hundreds of both major and minor muscles and joints in the body, it requires a great deal of energy, and this means that the heart and the lungs have to be working very well to achieve this. When kettlebell workouts are programmed in some sort of circuit, they will promote both strength and cardio performance simultaneously.

It is because of this that kettlebell training is gaining popularity as a tool that also saves time while generating more results. If you are a kettlebell workout beginner, one thing that you have to bear in mind is getting proper instructions from someone who is certified.

www.ingramcontent.com/pod-product-compliance
Lightning Source LLC
LaVergne TN
LVHW011951070526
838202LV00054B/4897